Dedicated to:

G d, the Universe,
& the unknown me

Quantum

IMMATERIAL

(Poetry from 2012 through 2013)

by Marisa Sachiko Keona Gasper

First Edition
Published on Lulu.com
2014

Poetry from 2012

To-day
7/21/12

**Note: I cannot say I did not in some ways appreciate my voyage through unspace/untime & illusion/unreality. This poem is about the experience and return from there, along with some of the ambivalence associated with currently living in reality, day to-day. I find this poem to be somewhat devoid of much feeling, for some reason...*

So the Every-day,
in normalcy bound (in unyielding case)

    burst
until its contents
lie askew –
                    disjointed, jaggedly jockeying in
                    pieces,
and
time suddenly passed
unhurriedly, though terrible in its
    disarray…

I am unable
to compute how
    sense was made
of cartoonish parts
    so hastily,
                    from one moment, in
                    minutiae.

The dramatic raising (follow, drop) of emotions,
seizures entwining practicality and pragmatics -
though matched: each one per…

One per: each Blinded By Illusion.

This then blending seams of sense,
trying to make cohesion stick -
                    from one point, scantily puzzling
                    definitions...

And my mouth spent rumbling mumbles,
my hands arranged in motion (in the air)
tracing fancies…

My mind made tricks
    of fear,
into obstructive delusions,
As if
        from each "need", desire became
            a *melting quagmire.*

And so,

I must now know things
which make no difference
to this society –
of day, to day… (but in space-less time make some meaning, perhaps?)?

…But,
why,
   No...

There is no *must*.

….Seems all there is to know is:
What *damage has been done?*

(on this trip…)

If this
savage, jumbled, ricocheting jungle
    of insane and baseless
thoughts, directions, and behaviors…
can now release into sudden recognition, semblance
of clarity
    and reality…
sewn into this day, to day…

...wondering if I may make it from
        madness
        to the next…

phase of scenes, rippling and settling…
(burbling quietly underneath all of the *fantasy*)

So, is it my wish
that I finally land in
what you or I
might call

Today?

(It may just be so, yes.
It may not be so, no.
It may bc just, maybc…)

It may be,

It may...

Increment Realized
7/25/12

A breath -
against windy torrents, the tremendous weight
of currents
affecting weather patterns
and rain

A fingerprint –
against swarming hands, the grabbing hustle
of people
touching items
repeatedly

A note –
against melodies, the thundering chorus
of voices
singing
as one

I look upwards to a sky
which has no anchor
in any particular
locale

I stand in a door among
a city boasting
doorways,
and windows, shuttered tight

I seek direction in a maze
of too many
options, then turn
steadily,

…as if I know…

I am silent,
and yearning,
fortified so.

I trace shadows
and run,
without footprint behind.

I stare steadily
and blink,
only when touched.

…We do not know
what it takes
for one to be
heard.

There are multitudes, against.

I find solace
while slipping unnoticed
in crowds.

I am singular

among
too many

to

count.

…But, I turn steadily,
and

there is *the only*

in

each

one.

Lonely
10/13/12

I'd have to say that even when I didn't feel lonely,
It wasn't that I was any less alone…

It was just that some other feeling somehow had more impact,
overshadowing the loneliness, for the time.

Poetry from 2013

"The only thing I know is the fact of my ignorance (Socrates)."
1/22/13

When knowledge limits you from further knowledge,
it is no longer
    useful.

Knowledge is not a game, or a contest.

It is not something on which
    to base
your
    worth.

Knowledge is not truth.
Truth is not knowledge.

That which is true is not something which passes some kind of test,
has no holes in it,
holds water
despite
the
attacks,
can be argued,
and sits
in
logical
    construct.

The search for truth and knowledge is often
pursued by those seeking power, control,
to "one-up" others, or even
to impress...

(And *I am not impressed*.)

Besides,
I would rather know
    why
someone does things,
than

who
or
what they

    “know.”

Ode to Erode Those 50-Cent Words
1/24/13

My intent is not to
    obscure and "poeticize"
when I communicate, but to
    explain
and

    illuminate.

Reluctant Awakening
2/1/13

I prefer an amalgam.
A multi-colored
    haze…

I want my ups, up -
and my downs, down.

For what most people would vote against,
I cheerfully swallow:
Anxiety
Despair
    Sorrow.

Despite all this,

it has become quiet
in my mind…

So much so
that each thought startles me

with its resounding
    announcement

As if to say, “I’m here! Let’s get this party started!”
(again).

But an unwavering solace
rests behind…

As if I could not drown,
though I try.

    I wish to

slumber peacefully.

But I find that I

    Awaken…

at
the
dawn.

"Betsy says I like Lofty Ideas"
3/31/13 (Mom’s Edit 4/5/13)

We are not
just energy
quantifiable, changeable, definable -

…Found in this world...

We are concepts that exist
    independent

(*Physicality is our infancy.*)

....We are beyond
material...

We are

    idea

in
   Form.

The Importance of Air: A Poem in Three Parts
(Subtitled: If Nothing is Something, then is Something but Nothing?
...And into thin air dispels our concern?)

(* Arrangement/Final Edit by MSKG & O. Leonelli)

I. The Void Expels…
5/5/13

What comes from nothing?
Twenty-one grams of animated dust?

The mass of energy is thus?
Life; identified
with flesh, in weight...?

"Super-organismal" creatures,
of differentiated cells -
whom are encoded, aggregated,
for whatever "purpose", are created.

Consciousness built upon masses,
    upon floor of multiple classes…
(And those, in plenty...
From more parts? Many…)

...We strange yet *walking* conglomerations...

We, these humans left:

...with even more impossible mysteries...
such incomprehensible histories,
such as:

"*There is no form to any force.*"
"*No trace of some things but in oblique.*"

Then we're messes with bellies of *emptiness*;
Distended and dry - gaseous hollowness;
Stuck with un-bubbled-in-answer-tests;
Quite quickly quixotic, lest *implying jest*?

Heads release (hot) air…
confess in gasps...

"These gaps -
we are bound to perceive..."

...So I fill them with my fantasy;
dreams full with *meaning* (and final, for me...)

In the breath before my eyes,
castles gleam -

Rainbow haze of vacillating...
as neurons, bright-firing, ever-out-reaching;
never-space-breaching - though racing, relating…

Like these (poignant plus plural)

Dimensions are waiting...

A kind of furthering -
from this world -> we create in,
an evolution -> elevating;
to Ever-increasing -> Never-abating...

…But,
from nothing did we come?
...And, to nothing shall we return?

I do not know...

The question still will learn (and churn...)
and burn...

until
  nothing

is
left

  to
  discern.

II. Meaning
4/25/13(Edited 5/5/13)

I thought she was joking when she replied,

I had asked earnestly, almost in
  angst:
"Why can we conceive of things which
  may not exist?"

And she said, "Air had a lot to do with it."

I thought she was
  joking.

But she explained (and I paraphrase): "When we discovered
that something upon which we depend to live,
was something we could not see..."

I finished the thought "…this allowed our imaginations to grow."

"And grow and grow…," she replied.

So easily - I could now -
see the logic inherent in human (d)evolution.

And I considered this - what had slighted my sight -

…This vague Vision I had for years… which so far was
based on - a bit of this…,
    a fancifully-constructed
Ideal - discarding that…,
creating worlds (beyond the visible) alighting in my mind,
illuminating made-real, fantasy-based desires

…though melded with
    meaning.

But this all-too-human conformity –
playing daydreams with afterlife, the Immaterial,
the intimation of improbable immortality…

So vacuous, and yet

    intimidating...
in
significance.

...So I ask you this: *Consider Meaning?*
And with all arguments that logic makes impossible,
Our ability to make sense out of something with our minds
does not necessarily make it true or false.

This flaw with logic, making it a closed-system game,
compares the loaded nature of my yearnings
to nothing more than something
    full of holes.

…But the necessity of hollowness is the embodiment of energy,
In emptiness is air, invisible, but we depend.

In *meaning*, there is so much more.

For what is our meaning?

…And why cannot neurons firing
(through space) ->
    make it up…?

…And,
from nothing did we come?
...And, to nothing shall we return?

I do not know...

The question still will learn (and churn...)
and burn...

until
    nothing

is
left

  to
  discern…

III. "Lungs"/Full
4/29/13(Edited 5/5/13)

Upon my last breath,
I shall awaken.
After falling into tunnel light,

Substantial slumber - but in a
    moment,
(and breathe again…)

Notice my translucence,
I am both replete, but still
    empty

Born complete (yet remiss of this)
Obsequious with innocence… and bliss,
Existence trysts with myth...

...I made it...
(to learn this new
    Dimension).

Fill air with color.

Shifting mazes of immaterial frame,
Entire worlds within gaze,
A footstep away.

There is hierarchy in eternity
making possible
ever-increasing understanding

With each expanse reached,
new comprehension seeps
into the depths of being.

This type of "Heaven"
unlike inscribed on page
…that sages forgot to whisper of,

That had raged within our fantasies,
Here, mere stage between life we knew –
From ages quivering in cages (of time),

And our histories, but gauge of worth,
Playing with name, and human girths -
Then body sound, material.

Full, full – was our reaching then,
To match the density of our surfaces,
Appearances were, for lack of better ways,

The ground on which to build your fame.

Dirt, and form…

Today, wings unfold,
the wind from lungs,
inflate – and fly.

Angel newness
made from

Meaning.

…So,
from nothing did we come?
...And, to nothing shall we return?

I do not know...

The question still will learn (and churn...)
and burn...

until
nothing

is
left

to
discern?

"The Dreaded OM"
5/2/13

Oh, OM…
"primordial sound of the Universe"
What yoga classes call forth thee?

What monks drone your monosyllabic hum…?

The round, warm yum
of your curved edges drown,
for feet yanked ungracefully beneath the knees…

Oh, please, fair OM,
What call forth thee?

Does the "Big Bang" resound
'tween the tongue
and the teeth?

Do the cosmos hang from the uvula?
Neatly arranged, circular droplets of sky -
sparkling,
bequeath needless grace - to empty space,
breathless black - around shimmering lakes,
the roar of black holes -
swallow thee,

Fear OM,
...whose noise awakens,
and deepens me…

For women enshrouded in spandex capris,
bodies rapt in postures bewildering me,
a mind in distraction (from all that it needs).

Oh, OM, oh dreaded OM,
What art thou, thee?

But a two-letter hail
to all that exists…
Mirroring then,
and the
    now,
in its infinite breadth…

Inhale,
and your sigh
does seem to
    emit,

A tale of the ages -
in
one
solemn
breath.

"Catastrophic Coverage"
5/3/13

Catastrophe is such a strong word.

…Made for furious weather,
natural disasters,
wartime destruction,
volcanic eruption.

There are small-time versions –
talk-show-worthy drama,
interpersonal altercation,
fights of inglorious fact,
mother's wrath.

…But to apply to round
and oblong shapes,
curved so as not to
cut the throats
of the ill,
purveyed by pharmacy,
fastidiously counted by technicians,

This seems an odd application –
In fact, a kind of modern distraction
from the reality of the infirm -
for this not applies to the sickness itself,
but to the stage insurance companies
slot you in –
to gauge how much they must pay.

For when in "catastrophic coverage"
You are 100% covered.

The scary thing is that I reach this point half-way through the year.

Medications so numerous and exorbitant to
catapult me into thus - so easily.
And am I so ill as to need this swill?

Well, apparently.

So ill it takes catastrophe to rear its ominous name,
that insurance companies merely nod their heads.

But I'm not dead,
and so I go about my days like
everyone else.

Epistemology
5/4/13

Her epistemology was "anarchic",
she said, "*there was no REAL knowledge of any kind.*"

…And I wondered what she took for granted,

at the time.

My Other Mother
5/7/13

I always remember the fruit
that she tenderly and skillfully packed,
…Not one, but many…
each in their zipper baggie,
or wrapped lovingly in a napkin.

Memories of overfull Easter baskets,
Over-generous Christmas gifts, the "too-good" food -

Traveling all over
in the back of her station wagon.

I remember how she cried when I got hit by a car
(when I was a Freshman in High School)
and how suddenly I realized she loved me…

And I think to myself,
how dutifully, how carefully she tends

her daughter… how even when she gets annoyed,
she continues to feed and change her.

And the other,
reared so wonderfully… becoming
a testament to her love, guidance,
and caring, (now a mother herself…)

She is grandmother to two,
whom she loves just as much.

I love her dearly.

…And as her hair is peppered with white…
I hold her idea in my mind as the
unconditionally
loving, supportive woman that she is.

An honest spirit… good, sweet,
thoughtful, and true…

Auntie E****… *this is You.*

Ode [in] Debt to The Flow
5/16/13

I owe a debt to her
    Flowing
Hair, for it surrounds her beauty -
shimmering, falling deftly
on the wind's whims...

Feel homage to her words'
    caress,
for their cradling,
adoring
tone...

P(r)ay toward her love,
for it is heavenly -

warm, G*d's nuzzle.

But a puzzle surely,
for her drama cries -
darkness awaiting her radiance -
just underneath the Awakening
bliss...

For this, my toll -
is lovingly paid, to
    Comfort
her in advance

...To assuage her fear of
- rocks in her river -

    Flow.

And,
hope she knows...?

I
Hope.

She

Knows.

Moola Mantra on a Friday Afternoon
5/17/13

Melody caresses the air,
gently kissing wafts -
breezes in notes…

Suddenly my voice raises
in song,

sacred words
awakening holy without…

and within,
waves of chills
begin near my knees –
in waterfall
upward
with the sound -

until I am overwhelmed,

and seek solace

in

thanks.

After Odette's "Ka Bloom!"
5/24/13

Explosion...
then expression of newness...

Like a Phoenix,
destruction, blooms.

Needy
5/20/13

Needy.

    Needy.

Greedy
for company.

Feeling a blank stare
in the

center of me.

A strain of anxiety
….fleeting…
from
    nowhere –
for no reason.

Reaching for a savior,

Needing
bodies warm wrapped.

Heeding no advice.

Led by the feeling…

Needy,

for

no

reason.

The Last Time I Considered Cliffs
5/20/13

I write this in order
for others to know
they are not
    alone.

That I have felt it too,
too many times to count.

That the dredge has dragged me
deep inside my center –
that darkness dwells within.

The last time I considered cliffs,
I was warm, at home, in bed.
Internally drove myself
to an all too familiar design.

A structure of always, and nevers,
Everythings, and nothings.
Destruction bound.

Again constructing “reasons”
to vacate this life.

Permanent vacation.

What always stopped me,
(when it was)
was fear of failure,
or that my mom’s friend was right:

That I would just have to repeat
The same thing,
The same way,
Until I made it through…

And it almost seems this happens anyway,
whether I live or die,

For the feeling comes for no reason sometimes –
….again and again and again…
spinning into a web of emotion,
misplaced,
but I always fail
and nothing ever comes through,
and never ever does everything turn out right.

Mood imbued
5/31/13

Unaware,
in meta-enmeshment,
I struggle with emotion.

Snare engaging,
Enraging,
I smuggle anger
(behind my intellect).

Danger does not blink,
Red seethes hot -
Sharp heat ringing the cage of
words caught within
(my absent stare).

Mood fluorescent,
Mood imbued...

The ascent of escalation -
descending into cascading
Depths, steps to nowhere,
emptiness where
Fear had filled me
Kills me, and

I am dead.

Somewhere Else
6/13/13

I'm going
    somewhere else

for the weekend.

Littering destinations
from either side of the windows.

Almost see - the
faraway look in eyes,
as
    wrist dismisses.

Nowhere to be found,
The loud distance.

Guilt
6/14/13

    Guilt
is
overrated.

Dated – (even).

Small “consolation” prize
for mislaid
    options.

…It is as if we shift
    concerns -

re-appropriate our energies,
(and then get out the lash…)

Coquettish
sadomasochistic
    tendencies
flirting
with great butterflies in gut playing

Tensions - building castles
in mind.

This is the fortress,
titlated and dressed by
stretched desires

making eyes messed.

Sirens sing verses
conversing in pet names
(in perverse hope, and frame)
to reverse
and assuage annoyance

At
My

    Self.

Faith looks like Diamonds (to her)
6/15/13

It's a pretty name, Faith,
brings to mind seemingly wholesome
light-haired girls
almost burgeoning with transparent
wings

Faith affords us each with a question: *What do you believe in?*

I wear a ring with "faith"
written in fonts fighting (with my style),
picking fight with personality

But it's not that I wonder WWJD,
I don't proclaim Jes*s Chr*st as my
Lord and Savior
for all to see.
It's not like I'm a good Chr*stian.
Of course, it's not like I'm not, either.
    I don't pray on my knees.

When I showed it to a friend,
she said that it sparkled like there were
diamonds in it.

And I cringed, explained why I wore it:

"I trust the Universe. I have faith that things will work out (in their own way) for everyone I know."

(It's a scary faith, not empty –
but not promised.)

The word sings - in
pentatonic scale
soaring harmonics
a frailty underwritten with strength
(Major made full with minor chords)

Faith in wintersummerfallspring,

faith in
good and bad, pain and pleasure, whatever fate brings...
faith in

everything.

Condescension Ascension
6/19/13

Minor chords on
stretchy heart strings
emotion played out, descending
in aria.

Looking down through a sneeze,
Insecurity reigns regal,
becoming "superiority", ascending
in tone.

Major chords proclaim
your entrance, fanfare -
and flash mobs, condescending
in balk.

I(n)

Mind.

Vogon Poem
6/19/13

Don't condescend to be my friend
If not up to standards thine
Or if you cannot understand
My few off moments in time

For I am human, flawed, and graced
Reaction bound, emotion laced...
With unshed tears upon my face
Ridiculous, and true...

Untitled
6/22/13

Slick,
and viscous,
slightly greasy,

your
    surface
neatly
gleams.

But I miss
the grit

which used to
sift, and mix, and

    texture

everything.

Maxine
7/1/13

She has the
biggest little eyes
I've ever seen,
her imploring "mew"
calling.

She was found wandering,
by herself, not quite 6 weeks old.

I heard she ate a bird
before I met her.

I could not help but
feel sorrow and tenderness
for this tiny kitten,
lonely,
abandoned by her mother,
lost amidst the city streets.

I cradled her in my hands,
a body too small for arms,
remarked at her sweet,
spunky soul.

She stalks over to my legs, brushing against them,
asking for a pet,
and love she missed.

"Maxine",
now a part of the
household.

A crew of three cats
and their "crazy cat lady"…

…Who smiles at me in the mirror -
any time

I take

a
glance.

Kitty Comforts Me
7/2/13

Kitty comforts me.
Her gray fur consoling,
Her white chest familiar,
Like home.

She bathes herself continually now,
As if perpetually dirty,
Concerned with staying clean.

She was looking rumpled for awhile,
As if she no longer cared,
As if she were ready to go to sleep...
(To dream of the eternal...)

But I asked her, please, to stay awhile, made her uncomfortable by wiping vitamin paste in her mouth,
Wanted to see her sleek and alive - again.

Her eyes are a little clearer now -
As if she's resigned herself to a few more years,
as if she's again okay with a cat's life.

And my gratitude grows -
as she settles in,
between my legs (for the night),
so we can sleep and dream -

The two who have spent so many nights,

Together.

~ Compass: A Poem in Four Directions ~

7/7-7/11/13

I. Compass: West

7/7/13

Then, you could stir
The darkness in me
With your index finger,
Clockwise, turn, (the old direction)
Counter, then a new inflection -
Shades of me you colored sullen
Mixing me with image, dulling...

...Got me every time,
for
In thine I placed
(The engine and the steering.)

But that history fades,
Twinkling only in your eye.

II. Compass: East

7/8/13

When the wind blows,
I am not lonely.

Howling does not raise the hair
On the back of my neck,
The wail sounding – serene of sorts

(Resounding in my memory.)

Clean,
and comforting.

…But I had walked the rows of classrooms, then,
with my eyes fixed on my feet –

As judgment passed,
Toes more friendly than passersby.

III. Compass: North
7/8/13

I reach, but not so high
(So as not to bump the ceiling)

Expectations do not trouble me.

I dwelled among the bottom feeders
Then, my status questionable -

For no one knew what to make
Of the scapegoat outcast,
Except to send their questionable to me
To make circles out of those who left...

I escaped the game we were all known to play,
Hierarchies unfathomable,
But obeyed nonetheless...

I called the Homecoming King by his proper name, scoffed at this title gleaming before all,

For I knew the darker sides of any game, and any throne,

For to fall or fail from any height
Is not a pleasurable
ride

down.

IV. Compass: South
7/11/13

A part of me had collected
Darkness from
Our greatest fears...
Bacteria, fungus, insects and incest In shadows terrifying,

Lying around in untended corners -
Unintended-horrors.

By themselves they had been merely untouchable, keep your hands clean of them, try to stay away,

But in groups they migrated South, you see, until they mingled with dirt and became filth and disease.

...My illness keeps part of me hidden away in the southern lands...
My addict temperament, depressive moments, times of chemical insanity, and then:
The wholeness of my soul...

For with the light that the mouth of the cave permits, I reach...
and
The part of me that is that light

can then

no longer

see...

The Euphoria of Toxicity
(Ode to the Good Old Days)
7/15/13

Oh, but to sweat with
profundity, as my body
works overtime to
purge paltry poisons picked
and put in purposely.

A wave of "Oh Shit!,"
my innards report.

But strangely, instead of fainting
or freaking out, my mind freezes

in euphoria.

I look around,
vaguely pleased with myself,
verbose
with
vacancy…

After Alice in Chains' "Nutshell"
7/17/13

I remember fearlessly entering
one of the very first chat rooms
that I found and went to - on the Internet -
when finally conceived.

It was a room of Alice in Chains' fans.

They spoke to each other
Entirely in Alice in Chains' lyrics,
    lyrical echoes –

and I was stunned by the depth
these words conveyed.

Rising up from under the dirt,
Flies dancing in errant array,
Magnificence trapped inside the words.

…And there's something about these chords,
that stir and strum the gut -

Shudder…

and warm, resonant
    strings and darkness,

drip
with oil

and

blood.

Amorphic "Amorals"
(Brief, Lazy Version)
7/30/13

In an atomic atmosphere,
Bits of ideation (idyllically)
Waft softly by

Darker, harder concepts… consume
And anomic anomalies animate

Though all judged as such,

Ornamentally in ordered array,
Orated in orange light,
Undulating in (underrated) understanding.

Amorphic "amorals"
(In algebraic arrangement)

They leverage loss,
And aggrandize gain,
And aggregate

Gross

Profits [sic],

for
"*Capitalism will eat its young…*" – Anonymous

After "Twinkle, Twinkle"
8/1/13

Twinkle twinkle little star

Why are you so goddamned far?
Though cosmos raped by Father Time
Still Mother Earth is so sublime…

Twinkle twinkle little star
Why are you so goddamned far?

The light at the end of the fairy tale
8/5/13

Tunnel vision
Born in libraries with
Even light

Spectacled girl less a spectacle
Reading, lost in story

Why was it that I loved fairy tales so?

They showed a light at the end of darkness
A reason to endure...

And this is why small children dreamed of glass slippers
And savior princes,
Of heroic fights for the princess' fate...

For the light at the end of the fairy tale meant

Happy
Days
Ahead.

The river underneath the myth
8/5/13

It flows
Meaning, in currents
It knows
Archetypal desire

It goes
From a mouth to an ear to a mouth again
It blows
The spirit out (from the body, and the mind)
It grows
(furiously churning)

…The low (splashing) burble
Gurgles and whispers
Warbles and twirls
Rushes and spills
Meddling and muddling
Cuddling and cradling…

We float
as the river takes hold of us
We gloat
As it mirrors the soul of us
We bloat
With recognition, as
We coat
ourselves in wet.

This is why a myth is mystery
Yet is mastery of history
(Subtly conditioning)
This is why a myth seeps into me
Is what I want to be
Is what is thought of me
This is why a myth comes through
From and then into (you)
(As if it knew you.)

As if the myth comes…

through

you.

Kitty's Purpose in Life
(Dedicated to my mother, Nancy)
8/22/13

"College is the dog collar on intelligence…" – O. Leonelli

How serene she curls
With tail in crescent
Round her svelte cat frame

Making home,
Softening spots
With the one-two, one-two – repeat
Pressing of paws into clothes piles

Her days are spent eating, drinking, sleeping,
Purring pets, and playing cat and mouse
With toys

One does wonder what life is to a cat.

But we puzzle over purpose,
Mull over meaning,
Daunted by the dilemma over what
"We're doing with our lives",
Live delirious with desire for destiny.

We question our quest,
Jockey our journey – to jive
With the jury

It's status we're after,
After all,
Masses of love, attention in our direction,
For why else yearn for more?

And do we question the purpose of the rich
Who spend their days shopping, and in leisure?
Do we wonder if what they do with their time is right?

Of course, no.

For purpose is a treasured trinket
Of the downtrodden,
Of the bourgeoisie,
Who must make point
Of their struggle,
Who must give reason
To their strife…

So I return to Kitty,
Who now naps soundly
(Sleeping 8-10 of her 13-18 year life)

Is she concerned with what's "going on" in her life?

Why, no.

For she simply is who she is.

None more much matters.

Nothing is but what you assign.

Reference points structured by society,
Perspective penned by proximity and affinity,
Preference a game,

"Purpose",

a

bane…

The Memory of Nothing
8/26/13

I relish
    unconsciousness

Though some may think sleep is a

Waste of time.

(Granted, I spend some of it dreaming.)

But nothing swirls
In concept,

Cold darkness, vacant vacuum,
Not-being-ness

Life is so full of that which is.

...What is this yearning?

What is my memory of
    Nothing?

Is this possible?

And will I know

    Nothing

Again?

"G d Morning Princess"
9/25/13

When did air
bite crimson sting
into my cheeks,
gazing unhurriedly
across the variant-vale?

Wind whip dark long waves
around my silver dress?

I forget these dreams.

I forget princes and knights,

kneeling before me.

When tadpole tails
evoked effervescent breath -
a promised kiss.

My heart used to
    flutter
then.

A Nice Guy with a Total Dick Education
(For Bobby King)
10/27/13

He laughs with mischief,
Says "sorry" with a smile.

Machiavelli siamesed with sincerity.

We were a garden in the heat,
Warm mix of mulch,
Decaying Matter.

His back is like a wave,
With his head turned,
Laughing into his armpits.

He wields shears,
Pruning fear
From leafless thorn.

But we are soft in the middle,
Tepid pool of water resting calm
Roots drinking.

He had spent weeks
Declaring his love for me.
Wiping soil on his apron,
Crafting bonsai from limbs
(which grown produce rafts)

Floating.

Advice to the Insecure
12/6/13

Escape is a peculiar "medicine"
Imbibe, inhale, intake, ingest
And don't forget the rest -
Any past-time passed sans -
A stable state of mind

Romanticism
surrounding
Ideas of self
(serve to quasi-liberate)

... Mental constructs abating panic -(when confronting
Actualities.)

The self-abuse standard,
Swinging pendulum -

Chattering mind.

So find:

...Instead of trying to get
people
to like you,

Try to get to like...

Yourself.

The Bar is not a Coping Skill

12/10 & 12/13/13

The bar is not a
Coping skill

Can't drink that crap away

There may be much
To run from

But it's only on
Delay.

Acceptance

12/16/13

Acceptance is intoxicating
Almost
    Unconditional love

Like a mother
Detoxifying
The world's hurts.

Who will love this damaged
    reflection -

Ending in a question mark – indelicately

What pairs do speak in almost whispers
The
care
    unknown before.

Ridiculous
12/16/13

The farce of my life
Is based on numbers
Set then
And noticed since

Their significance
Was purely personal

Like anything, and superstitious
Coincidence

But now that age
Makes a Mark in my calendar

You knock it down
With words
That run

And the numbers crumble
With the years I loved you

To Nothing,
As it was based upon

From Catharsis to Cathexis
12/17/13

Purge willingly
That which ails you

It has haunted inside
Of your skin

Like a disease – if "love" curtails you
(From any other whim)

…Then meaning rears its head

Again,

Roar to wail…
(Such a heavenly sin.)

To place your hopes in
Yet another one

And let the new game, then,

Begin.

Things aren't suddenly over
(When you decide they are)
12/18/13

"*I'm the 'decider', I make the decisions…*"

…So said the big head
leading the country,

Masculinity,
at its finest.

And so follows…

When you decide you're done,
After I've dealt with your sour
Pungency,
The yelling, and the blame,
The frightening postures,
The preposterous posturing,
The sneers
(And more of the same…)

It's suddenly over?

(As if it were never there?)

No.

I don't think so.

For,

Where is the
     fallout
from this
     nuclear
imposition?

Who has felt the blast from your words?
Who wears scars from your shrapnel expressions?
Who is both cowering (and angry herself) now
for enduring
Your darkest yet
blinding wrath?

Why, I am.

And no, things aren't suddenly over

When you're ready for them to be.

Consequences
Sting.

…And while they will never
Measure up to the outburst,

You will feel
A bit
Of the pain

You have
caused

Me.

OCD, HPD, and NPD become BPD, then finally, ASPD
12/19/13

I'm going to call on my behavioral disorder tendencies
And split.

I'm going to stop caring
And feel nothing.

I'm going to skate the boundaries
Of insanity - but only in a sociopathic way.

You see, I'm on my way...

You know,
They should make psych wards
For scorned women

Where they can learn to employ their disorders in expedient fashion

Where they can scream their heads off

And learn not to feel...

So as never to be hurt

Again.

Bobby's Nannie
12/29/13

"You want to get rid of him for a couple of days," she said,
Matter of fact, almost with a smile...

So to the point.

She loved in reality,
Saw what was and
Allowed it.

And another time, "He don't want to admit he f***ed up yet," imploring with me
To forgive him.

She was a whip
fit with feathers,

A soft waft of
hard truth

A flower in the harsh light

Of day.

She did what she wanted until
Her dying wish was
Satisfied.

She was color, yet traced in black and white.

Enjoyed her salt, her cigarettes, and
The taste of sugar.

She was
A woman...

With many names.

ISBN 978-1-304-78732-3

www.ingramcontent.com/pod-product-compliance
Ingram Content Group UK Ltd.
Pitfield, Milton Keynes, MK11 3LW, UK
UKHW041840200726
13854UKWH00003BA/1234